HE HAS SHOT THE PRESIDENT!

THE DAY JOHN WILKES BOOTH KILLED PRESIDENT LINCOLN

Actual Times

VOLUME FIVE — APRIL 14, 1865 — $17.99

HE HAS SHOT THE PRESIDENT!

BY DON BROWN

ROARING BROOK PRESS
New York

In memory of Aunt Rita

1914–2013

Greatly loved, greatly missed

Copyright © 2014 by Don Brown
Published by Roaring Brook Press
Roaring Brook Press is a division of Holtzbrinck Publishing Holdings Limited Partnership
175 Fifth Avenue, New York, New York 10010
mackids.com

Library of Congress Cataloging-in-Publication Data

Brown, Don, 1949–
  He has shot the president! : April 14, 1865 : the day John Wilkes Booth killed President Lincoln / By Don Brown.
    pages cm.—(Actual times ; volume 5)
  ISBN 978-1-59643-224-6 (hardcover)
1. Lincoln, Abraham, 1809–1865—Assassination. 2. Booth, John Wilkes, 1838–1865. I. Title.
  E457.5.B86 2014
973.7092—dc23

2013016334

Roaring Brook Press books may be purchased for business or promotional use. For information on bulk purchases please contact Macmillan Corporate and Premium Sales Department at (800) 221-7945 x5442 or by email at specialmarkets@macmillan.com.

First edition 2014
Book design by Andrew Arnold
Printed in China by Toppan Leefung Printing Ltd., Dongguan City, Guangdong Province

1 3 5 7 9 10 8 6 4 2

Washington, D.C., April 14, 1865

t was a rare, cheerful day for
President Abraham Lincoln.

The burdens of waging a bitter four-year civil war were lifting. Destruction of the southern states' Confederacy was near. Lincoln had reason to feel lighthearted. He had held the United States together and abolished slavery.

Not far from the White House, another man considered the outcome of the war. For this man the looming Confederate defeat was a monstrous injustice engineered by the tyrant Abraham Lincoln. It filled him with seething rage.

The man was John Wilkes Booth.

By day's end, circumstances—some by chance and some manufactured—placed the two men together, and in that doleful moment, murder followed.

President Lincoln began his day by meeting with other government leaders, including his commanding general, Ulysses S. Grant. He had a quiet day planned: paperwork and a carriage ride in the afternoon, followed by an evening with Mrs. Lincoln and friends at the popular Ford's Theater.

John Wilkes Booth began his day by stopping by the same Ford's Theater. He was a popular and handsome actor who regularly performed there, and it was a place he could relax and gossip. This morning he heard that President Lincoln would be attending the evening performance.

Booth defended slavery and supported the South's independence. He despised Lincoln and declared, "He is made a tool of the North, to crush out slavery, by robbery, rapine, slaughter, and bought armies."

Instead of joining the battle as a soldier with the Confederate army, Booth concocted a plan to end the fighting by kidnapping President Lincoln and delivering him to Confederate leaders. By 1864, Booth had collected a handful of like-minded people who plotted and schemed but never acted. All the while, the Confederacy collapsed. The great Confederate general Robert E. Lee surrendered. And Booth boiled.

His mind now turned to killing Lincoln. He believed that robbing the Union of the president's leadership would cripple the North and save the South. When he heard the news of Lincoln's visit to Ford's Theater, Booth saw a chance to murder the president in a grand setting. "It would be the greatest thing in the world!" Booth said.

That afternoon, he whispered his murder scheme to some members of his kidnapping gang. To heighten the damage to the Union, Booth also proposed killing Vice President Andrew Johnson and Secretary of State William Seward. While some who heard the idea wanted no part of it, Lewis Powell, David Herold, George Atzerodt, and widow Mary Surratt agreed.

Lewis
Powell

David
Herold

George
Atzerodt

Mary
Surratt

Booth then went to Mary Surratt's boardinghouse. Mary's son, John, was another of Booth's kidnapping gang but was in Canada working as a Confederate spy. On Booth's instructions, the widow went to a nearby Maryland tavern that she owned and delivered a package of the actor's guns to the care of the tavern keeper. She told the keeper to "have those shooting irons ready that night— there might be some parties call for them."

Back at Ford's Theater, owner Harry Ford set up the president's box, a small space separated from the balcony seats by a narrow passageway, a vestibule, and two doors. He placed seats in the box, including a walnut rocking chair for Lincoln. Ford decorated the outside of the box with American flags, a blue Treasury flag, and a large framed portrait of George Washington.

Sometime that day, Booth sneaked into the box and hid a wooden bar he planned to later use as a door jam.

Meanwhile, Abraham and Mary Lincoln had enjoyed their afternoon carriage ride. His good humor prompted Mrs. Lincoln to say, "Dear Husband, you almost startle me by your cheerfulness."

They arrived at Ford's at 8:30 PM. With them were Major Henry Rathbone and his bride-to-be Clara Harris. The play, *Our American Cousin,* had already started. The couples sat in a row, with Lincoln directly beside the vestibule door. There were no armed guards.

Downstairs, Booth arrived in the alley behind Ford's Theater on his horse. Hidden on the actor was a small, single-shot derringer pistol and a large knife. He entered the rear of Ford's, leaving his horse in the care of a theater worker, and then sneaked to the front where he exited and made a brief visit to a neighboring saloon.

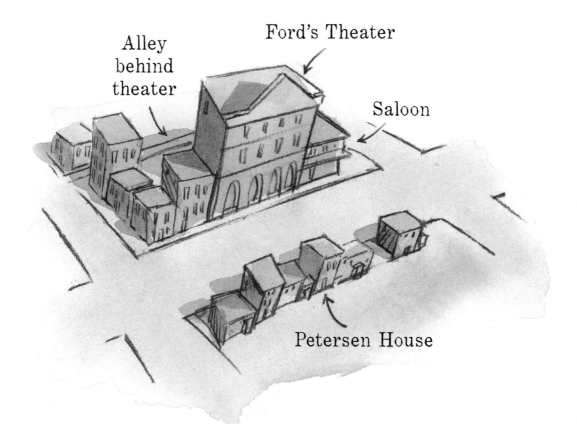

Alley behind theater

Ford's Theater

Saloon

Petersen House

At about 10:00 PM, Booth reentered Ford's through the front entrance and made his way to the second floor and the president's box. Blocking the door to the box was Lincoln's valet and helper, Charles Forbes. The arrival of the actor did not alarm Forbes. Instead he allowed Booth to enter to the vestibule outside Lincoln's box.

Once inside the tiny vestibule, Booth jammed the door with the wooden bar he'd hidden earlier, effectively locking Forbes outside. No one would be able to disturb him now.

Booth waited.

He was familiar with the play and knew a funny scene was coming. Booth listened to the two actors on stage banter until the comic line arrived. When the audience erupted with laughter, Booth silently slipped into the president's box and pressed the small pistol to the back of Lincoln's head. He squeezed the trigger.

Flash!

Bang!

A round lead bullet sliced through the president's skull, stopping behind his right eye.

The shocked Major Rathbone jumped up from his seat to the right of President and Mrs. Lincoln and wrestled with the assassin. But Booth stabbed the major's arm and leaped from the box toward the stage below. One of Booth's riding spurs caught on the box's decorative flags, and he made a clumsy, crouched landing.

With a burst of energy, Booth sprang up, raised the knife above his head, and thundered, *Sic semper tyrannis!*—"Thus always to tyrants!"

Then, with a triumphant shout of "The South is avenged," he raced off stage toward the theater's back exit. No audience member, actor, or stagehand tried to stop Booth. Everyone was stunned and confused.

"Was that part of the play?" some people wondered.

Rathbone and his fiancée, Clara Harris, cried, "Stop that man! He has shot the president!"

But it was too late. Booth mounted his waiting horse and vanished into the night.

Meanwhile, gang member Lewis Powell arrived at the home of Secretary of State William Seward, who was mending from a near-fatal carriage accident nine days earlier. Hidden in Powell's clothes were a knife and a revolver. Claiming to have medicine for the secretary, Powell tried to enter the secretary's sickroom. But Seward's grown son, Frederick, ordered him out. Suddenly, Powell pulled a revolver from his long coat, aimed it inches from Frederick's face, and pulled the trigger.

Nothing!

The revolver had misfired.

But the solidly built Powell used the gun as a club to hammer Frederick senseless.

Powell then rushed into Secretary Seward's room and came face-to-face with Seward's twenty-year-old daughter, Fanny, and his nurse, Army Sergeant George Robinson.

Powell stabbed Robinson and raced to the secretary's bed where the broken-boned and immobile Seward lay. Fanny threw herself in Powell's way, but he pushed her aside.

"Don't kill him!" she yelled.

Powell stabbed Secretary Seward.

Once.

Twice.

Blood flew.

Fanny howled in horror.

Somehow the injured Robinson recovered and jumped on Powell. The two men fought for their lives.

The ruckus woke Seward's other grown son, Gus, who had been sleeping in a neighboring room. He joined the struggle.

Grappling now with two men, Powell stabbed Robinson twice in the shoulder and then broke free.

"I'm mad. I'm mad!" Powell cried, as if offering some kind of strange confession.

Barreling from the house, he met and stabbed an unfortunate government messenger who'd just arrived on a routine visit.

Back in the bedroom, Robinson ignored his own injuries and rushed to the bloody pile that was William Seward.

"I am not dead," Seward painfully whispered. "Send for a doctor, send for the police, close the house."

Lincoln shot. Seward stabbed. What of the third target, Vice President Andrew Johnson?

He rested peacefully at his temporary hotel residence. At the hotel's bar, his intended assassin, George Atzerodt, got drunk. Neither sober nor bold, he wandered away.

Blocks away at Ford's Theater, there was chaos.

"What has happened?" the crowd screamed.

"Has the president been shot?"

"Catch him! Kill the murderer!"

"Is there a doctor in the house?"

Army surgeon Dr. Charles Leale hurdled theater seats as he rushed to the president's box. Moments passed until the jammed door was freed and the doctor reached Lincoln. The president sat slumped over.

Mary Lincoln moaned, "Father. Father. Oh, my dear husband."

From below, another doctor climbed up a flag and into the front of the box to join Leale. A third doctor arrived.

Lincoln lived, but barely. The doctors laid him flat. Leale searched for the wound and found a small hole behind the president's left ear. Leale said, "His wound is mortal; it is impossible for him to recover."

The three doctors decided to move the president to a safer, more comfortable place. While they held Lincoln's head and shoulders, four soldiers from the audience carried Lincoln into the street. The grief-stricken crowd outside made a corridor for them to pass. From across the street, a boarder at the Petersen House called, "Bring him in here, bring him in here."

They carried Lincoln into a rear room and onto a bed. It was too short for the six foot four president, and even laid diagonally his feet hung off the end.

Meanwhile, Booth galloped out of Washington.

Traveling ahead of the assassination news, he crossed a bridge to Maryland with little interference from the soldier guard. Following moments behind him was coconspirator, David Herold. Earlier, Herold had the job of holding Powell's horse during the murder of Secretary Seward. But Fanny Seward's screams had frightened him away. He had abandoned Powell and raced out of the city to meet Booth. The gang's plan was for Herold to be the actor's guide through Maryland and to the safety of the South.

On the dark road, Booth and Herold met.

They stopped at Mary Surratt's tavern and collected guns, ammunition, and binoculars from the keeper. They asked about a doctor—Booth had broken his leg during the clumsy fall from the president's box. But the keeper knew of none. Before dashing away, Booth made a proud, if not wholly correct, announcement, "We have assassinated the president and Secretary Seward."

In Washington, a knot of people stood a grim deathwatch around Abraham Lincoln. Newly summoned doctors, Lincoln's eldest son, Robert, and government leaders, including Secretary of War Edwin Stanton, all gathered to wait and pray. Stanton had helped Lincoln steer the nation through the bloody war and was perhaps the second most powerful man in the country. This fierce and ruthless man took over the powers of the president and no one, not even Vice President Andrew Johnson, objected.

Edwin Stanton

From news brought to the Petersen House, Stanton quickly learned that Lincoln's assassin was John Wilkes Booth. He vowed to capture Booth and all who had helped him. Stanton sent telegrams to the military and the police to be on the lookout; it was the start of a great manhunt.

Meanwhile in Maryland, Booth and Herold awakened the household of Dr. Samuel Mudd.

The doctor set Booth's broken leg with splints and invited the tired men to rest in a second-floor bedroom.

As they slept, Lincoln's strength slipped away. Finally, at 7:22 AM, April 15, he drew no more breaths and his heart stopped. President Abraham Lincoln was dead.

"Now he belongs to the angels," said a tearful Edwin Stanton.

Lincoln's body was wrapped in
an American flag and taken to the
White House.

When Lincoln died, Booth and Herold were resting at Dr. Mudd's. Later that day, the doctor attended to business in a nearby town and encountered cavalrymen hunting Lincoln's assassin. But he told them nothing of his two peculiar nighttime visitors. Instead, Mudd returned home and asked Herold and Booth to leave. He directed them to Samuel Cox, a Confederate sympathizer, who agreed to help them across the Potomac River to Virginia. The two fugitives went to nearby woods to hide.

Cox enlisted Confederate agent Thomas Jones, a veteran of many dangerous secret missions, to help Booth and Herold. Jones found the two men in a pine thicket and explained, "You must stay right here, however long, and wait till I can see some way to get you out."

In Washington, grief-stricken citizens draped the capital in black. News of the president's death brought grief and rage. In the days that followed, some people caught gloating over the murder were beaten, hung, or shot. Perhaps hundreds died.

Investigators searched for Booth and all who helped him.

Mary Surratt's strong connection to John Wilkes Booth earned her questioning from detectives just hours after the president's attack. On April 17, she was arrested. As authorities were leading Mary Surratt out of her home, a large stranger appeared at the door. Since he was unable to explain his visit, soldiers took the mysterious man to jail as well. The big man was Seward's attacker, Lewis Powell.

Powell and Surratt were just two of many people grabbed by the authorities in their relentless, sweeping investigation. George Atzerodt was captured in Maryland. Hundreds were arrested, including all the boarders at the Surratt House; even eleven-year-old Appolina Dean was taken and briefly held.

The story of Dr. Mudd and his two mysterious visitors eventually became known to investigators. He insisted he merely cared for the strangers.

"I never saw either . . . before . . . nor can I conceive who sent them to my house," he protested.

But at later questioning, he admitted knowing the actor. Mudd was arrested.

Had Dr. Mudd knowingly aided Abraham Lincoln's killer?

And still the nation wondered, "Where was John Wilkes Booth?"

While the search went on, heartbroken Americans paid Abraham Lincoln their last respects. On the morning of April 19, a crash of cannons announced Lincoln's funeral. The guns would roar regularly throughout the day. Six grand white horses drew the president's body to the Capitol's Rotunda. Five thousand people marched in the procession, all led by the Twenty-second Regiment of the United States Colored Troops. Tens of thousands watched the mournful parade. The next day, thousands upon thousands streamed into the Rotunda and filed past the president's body.

That same day, Secretary of War Stanton offered a $100,000 reward for the capture of John Wilkes Booth.

"Let the stain of innocent blood be removed from the land by the arrest and punishment of the murderers," Stanton said. "All good citizens are exhorted . . . to rest neither day or night until it is accomplished."

On April 21, a special train carrying Lincoln's body departed Washington headed for his hometown of Springfield, Illinois. The train followed roughly the same path Lincoln had taken to the Capitol for his inauguration four years earlier. Slowly leaving the station, it passed members of the Eighth United States Colored Artillery. A voice called, "Good-bye, Father Abraham."

At funeral honors in New York City, people filed past the casket for twenty-five hours, yet satisfying only a small portion of the half million people waiting to view the body. Afterward, an enormous procession followed the coffin back to the train. City leaders tried to prevent African Americans from taking part, but Secretary Stanton telegraphed from Washington "that no discrimination respecting color be exercised," and the prohibition was removed.

Millions viewed the dead president at funeral stops or stood vigils for a glimpse of the slowly moving train that carried him home. By the time Lincoln reached Springfield, one in four of all Americans had paid their respects.

All the while Booth and Herold hid in the thick and chilly Maryland woods. Thomas Jones regularly visited them and brought them food. After five days and four nights, he finally decided, "The coast is clear."

He led them to a small boat on the Potomac River and gave them directions to a creek in Virginia on the opposite shore.

"Mrs. Quesenberry lives near the mouth of this creek. If you tell her you come from me I think she will take care of you," Jones said, pushing the boat into the current of the black river.

But the dark water and moonless night proved too unsettling for Booth, and even using the compass he carried, they veered off course. After hours of exhausting rowing by Herold, they landed the boat . . . near where they started in Maryland!

Luck placed them near the home of a friend of Herold's, who fed the two tired fugitives and allowed them to hide on his property.

After two days hiding on the riverbank, Booth and Herold made a second try for Virginia.

As they paddled downstream, a Union gunboat appeared!

They barely sneaked passed and landed in Virginia. The agreeable Mrs. Quesenberry arranged for help getting them south.

Nine days had passed since Lincoln had been shot.

Since Booth's broken leg made riding difficult, they hired a wagon. Reaching Port Conroy on the Rappahannock River, they encountered three young Confederate cavalrymen.

To the trio, Herold confessed, "We are the assassinators of the president. Yonder is the assassinator! Yonder is J. Wilkes Booth, the man who killed the president!"

The soldiers and fugitives joined up and crossed the Rappahannock together. The group found their way to the farm of Richard Garrett where Booth and Herold pretended to be Confederate veterans traveling home.

The hot food and a clean bed were a sharp improvement from the rough life Booth had been living since the assassination. But despite the apparent good fortune, his luck had turned very, very sour.

Investigators in Washington had received news that two men in a small boat had been seen crossing the Potomac River. They decided the reported men must be Booth and Herold, and two detectives and a company of cavalrymen were ordered to race after them.

The authorities had no idea that the new hunt was for the *wrong* men.

The reported river crossing of the two suspected men had occurred before Booth and Herold's trip. But in a bizarre twist of luck, the hard-riding manhunters weren't on a wild-goose chase; they had been ordered to a corner of Virginia that was home to the Garrett farm and the comfortably resting John Wilkes Booth!

On April 25, the detectives and cavalrymen arrived at Port Conroy and picked up Booth's trail. They discovered that Booth had crossed the river in the company of three Confederate soldiers, were given the identity of the soldiers, and learned that one of the soldiers—Willie Jett—was courting an innkeeper's daughter in a neighboring town.

The searchers immediately started off at a gallop down the road. Might Booth be with Jett at the inn?

Two of the rebels who had teamed up with Booth and Herold were on the road, visiting a nearby town, when they spotted the approaching Yankee horsemen. They slipped past the Union men unnoticed and raced to the Garrett farm to warn Booth and Herold. They all hid as the unknowing cavalrymen raced past the farm toward the inn in town.

The Yankees reached the inn late that night and discovered Jett. In moments, the rebel had a Union revolver pointed at his temple. He stammered, "I know who you want, and I will tell you where they can be found."

With Jett as a guide to the Garrett farm, the manhunters closed in on the most wanted man in America.

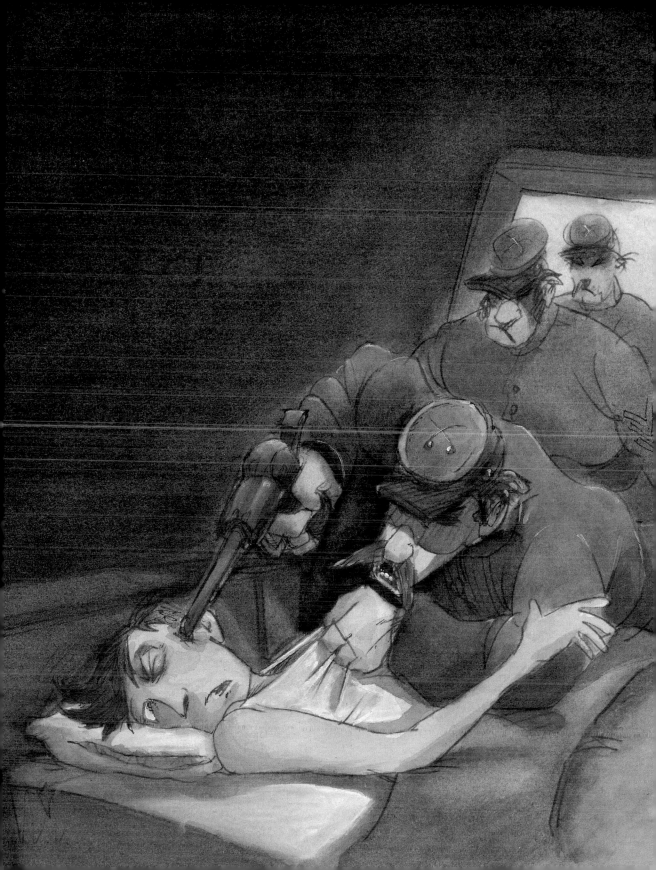

At the farm, the shock of the thundering Union horsemen and Booth and Herold's alarm had given the Garretts pause. Who were these men they were helping? Were they a threat to the family?

As a precaution, the Garretts ordered Booth and Herold to sleep in the farm's tobacco barn. To stop them from possibly stealing one of family's horses in the middle of the night, the Garretts secretly locked the door behind them.

At 2:00 AM on the morning of April 26, heavy fists of Yankee cavalrymen pounded the Garretts' door.

After twelve days, the reckoning for Abraham Lincoln's murder had finally arrived.

"Where are the men that were here today?" the cavalrymen barked.

John Garrett, one the Garretts' grown sons, revealed the fugitives' hiding place. The soldiers surrounded the barn and ordered John to demand Booth's surrender.

The commotion of the Yankee's arrival had awakened Booth and Herold. They tried to flee and discovered the locked door.

"You had better give up," Herold said.

"I will suffer death first," Booth replied.

The trapped men retreated into the darkness of the barn. John Garrett entered and tried to convince the cornered men to surrender.

From outside, an impatient detective threatened to burn the barn if Booth didn't give up.

Garrett fled.

But the stubborn Booth refused to surrender.

He shouted, "I am nothing but a cripple. I have but one leg, and you ought to give me the chance for a fair fight."

The barn was set ablaze.

Peering through cracks between the barn's wall slats, Booth could be seen in the fire's pulsing light armed with rifle and handgun.

Union Sergeant Boston Corbett trained his revolver on Booth. As Booth raised his rifle, Corbett fired.

Booth threw up his hands and collapsed.

The two detectives rushed forward and dragged Booth from the burning barn.

Corbett's shot had pierced Booth's neck. The wound brought him great agony.

"Kill me!" he moaned. "Kill me!"

Hours passed. As the sun rose, John Wilkes Booth died.

The chase for America's most-wanted villain was over.

His body was returned to Washington and buried in a secret unmarked grave at the Old Arsenal army post.

That summer, Booth's fellow gang members were convicted for their part in the Lincoln assassination.

The dishonest Dr. Mudd was sentenced to life imprisonment for aiding the assassin.

Mary Surratt, Lewis Powell, George Atzerodt, and David Herold were sentenced to death by hanging.

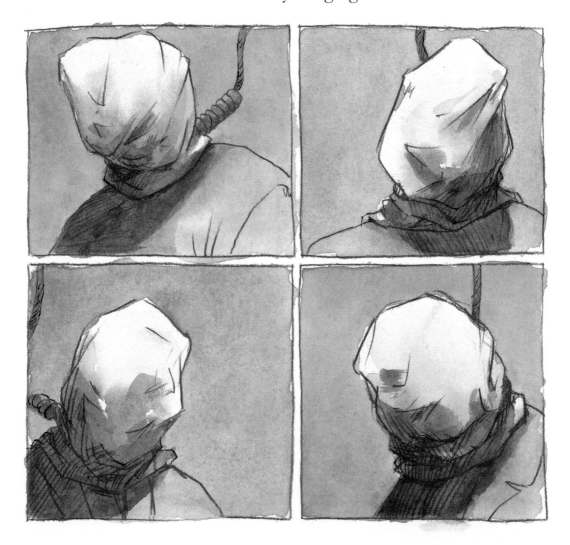

On July 7, 1865, the four condemned prisoners climbed a common scaffold and stepped onto a platform with large trapdoors. They were bound with strips of white linen and had cotton hoods placed over their heads. Rope was tied around their necks. The hangman clapped his hands three times and soldiers beneath the scaffold released the trapdoors. The great crime came to a grisly end.

And with it, the bloody Civil War also drew to a close. William Seward recovered, though scarred, and returned to his secretary of state post. He is remembered today for promoting the purchase of Alaska from Russia in 1867. Edwin Stanton remained secretary of war but clashed with President Johnson over the best ways to reconstruct the South.

Booth had failed. The president's murder didn't save the Confederacy. Victory belonged to the Union, and a United States of America reemerged.

In 1869, the government released Booth's body from his secret grave and returned it to his family. He was buried in the Booth family plot in Green Mount Cemetery in Baltimore, Maryland. He lies there still.

But don't look for his name; it's absent from the marker.

Bibliography

Kauffman, Michael W. *American Brutus: John Wilkes Booth and the Lincoln Conspiracies.* New York: Random House, 2004.

Steers, Edward Jr. *Blood on the Moon: The Assassination of Abraham Lincoln.* Lexington, KY: University Press of Kentucky, 2001.

Swanson, James L. *Manhunt: The 12-Day Chase for Lincoln's Killer.* New York, Harper Perennial, 2006.